ASYLUM

Inside the Pauper Lunatic Asylums

Mark Davis

AMBERLEY

First published 2014

Amberley Publishing
The Hill, Stroud
Gloucestershire, GL5 4EP

www.amberley-books.com

ISBN 978 1 4456 3614 6 (print)
ISBN 978 1 4456 3642 9 (ebook)

British Library Cataloguing in
Publication Data.
A catalogue record for this book is
available from the British Library.

Typesetting by Amberley Publishing.
Printed in the UK.

CONTENTS

Acknowledgements   4

Introduction   5

Staffordshire County Asylum   11

West Riding Pauper Lunatic Asylum   19

Cheshire County Pauper Lunatic Asylum   25

North Wales County Pauper Lunatic Asylum   31

Eglington Pauper Lunatic Asylum   43

Lincolnshire County Pauper Lunatic Asylum   49

Northumberland County Pauper Lunatic Asylum   57

Surrey County Pauper Lunatic Asylum   67

West Riding Pauper Lunatic Asylum   77

Lanark District Pauper Lunatic Asylum   87

Glasgow District Pauper Lunatic Asylum   97

St Kevin's Pauper Lunatic Asylum   103

East Sussex County Pauper Lunatic Asylum   111

Brecon & Radnor Joint Counties Pauper Lunatic Asylum   119

Gateshead Borough Pauper Lunatic Asylum   127

West Park Mental Hosptial   137

Barrow Gurney Mental Hospital   155

ACKNOWLEDGEMENTS

For historical information abandonedireland.com, whateversleft.co.uk, thetimechamber.co.uk, highroydshospital.com, wakefieldasylum.co.uk

For being a rock, Louise Irving and Alice Rose.
  This book is dedicated to my son, Benjamin Davis, who has battled through adversity and come out a champion.

INTRODUCTION

'There they stand, isolated, majestic, imperious, brooded over by the gigantic water-tower and chimney combined, rising unmistakable and daunting out of the countryside – the asylums which our forefathers built with such immense solidity to express the notions of their day. Do not for a moment underestimate their powers of resistance to our assault.'

– As said by the then Government Health Minister Enoch Powell in March 1961 when he made the first steps to make these once self-contained villages for the insane a thing of the past.

Once a familiar landmark of the British landscape, the old Victorian asylums were places where legends were created. They were places of mystery where, according to folk, 'all sorts went on'. Even schoolchildren in the playground would taunt each other with, 'You're mental! You're off to Menston' – referencing High Royds Psychiatric Hospital. Such phrases as 'going round the bend' originate from the fact that many an asylum could be found at the top of an impressive curved drive, effectively hiding the institution from the prying eye of the inquisitive public.

In the nineteenth century, reception into the asylum was potentially the beginning of an arbitrary life sentence in one of many large, seventy-bed dormitories. To some it was worse than going to prison; at least with a prison you had a release date. At the asylum there was only a 30–50 per cent discharge rate. As a rule, the asylum would be located in relative isolation within reasonable distance from the local town and railway.

During the latter part of the nineteenth century, county asylums were built at a rapid rate to cater for society's intolerance to behaviour and the increasing human wreckage associated with the newly industrialised society. The patient population was drawn primarily from the despised pauper class, although limited numbers of private paying patients were admitted. The majority of paupers were direct transfers from the workhouse union (referred to in Bradford by the poor as the 'Bastille') and the magistrates' court upon the recommendation of the police doctor. The patients, or inmates as they were referred to, came from all walks of life, although the biggest percentage were of the unskilled class such as labourers or mill workers. However, it was not unheard of for a policeman or even a schoolmaster to be admitted under the banner of care and treatment.

When researching the nineteenth-century patient, it soon becomes clear that the noted probable cause of insanity and how that cause manifests itself can appear worlds apart. For example, in the case of one patient, a young woman of twenty-eight, the supposed cause was 'conflict with husband'. In reality, she had GPI (general paralysis of the insane), the conflict being her husband had infected her with syphilis. Inmates with GPI accounted for a good proportion of the asylum population, as did the manic, the depressed and the intemperate.

Treatment for the Victorian patient ranged from opium as the main sedative in the mid-nineteenth century to laudanum, bromide, and chloral hydrate, while physical treatment included Turkish or hot baths, wet sheet packs and electric stimulation. Staff were invariably employed from the local population. Thus, in time, small local towns grew with generations of families being employed. Experience in those early days was not required: quite simply if you were physically fit and either a good sportsman or able to play a musical instrument then you were very likely to be offered a position on the staff.

Times have certainly moved on: the stigma of mental health is a mere shadow of itself in 2014 compared to Victorian intolerance, where families would disown a relative for fear of themselves being labelled insane. Many believed insanity was hereditary.

Right: The author in Menston Asylum water tower.
(*Image by Mike Bottomley*)

It is very easy to demonise these institutions, but in order to get a better understanding one needs to remove the age-old preconceptions. Certainly it's true that for some people life in the asylum represented a living hell, but for others there came an acceptance and tolerance and with that a quality of life. It is wise to remember that no one is immune from mental illness. It can happen in one form or another to anyone at anytime.

Through this book, which features seventeen former asylums and mental hospitals, we take a look at this hidden world and visit the corridors and dormitories where thousands of people lived out their lives under treatment. The pictures take us to a world far removed from our own where we can justifiably breath a sigh of relief and be thankful that the days of possibility of incarceration in a lunatic asylum are over...

A Contemporary Account of the Victorian Asylum

WAKEFIELD PAUPER LUNATIC ASYLUM REPORT 1849

The completion during the past year of the New Building, with the consequent changes and improvements have made the Institution sufficiently fitted to the purpose for which an Asylum is intended.

Accommodation is now provided for all applicants made for admission, and means afforded for a more improved classification of the Patients; and greater comfort has been provided by increased space, improved ventilation and warming, with a light and cheerful locality.

As regards the general principles on which the Institution is conducted, no material alteration has been found necessary. The addition of a large auxiliary building has required some changes in the domestic arrangements; such as the removal of the Assistant Matron and the House Surgeon from their residence in the Old Building to the apartments provided for them in the New Year; as also the adoption of the convenience furnished in the newly built laundry, bake house, and brew house. All matters of merely domestic economy have been adapted to the requirements of the two Institutions. Moral and medical treatment has been a continuous system founded as long tried principles.

So large a number of admissions has not in any former period appeared in the annual reports. Of the 257 admitted during the last year, 118 were males, 139 females. Many townships have sent, at once, the whole number of their insane paupers, who had been placed in various private houses until the enlargement of the Asylum rendered it fit for their reception.

In such an influx of hopeless cases, the prospect of cure must have been very faint, whilst in many instances it was but too apparent that the patient was merely admitted to die. Many of the friends of such patients have warmly expressed their gratitude for the care and attention the sufferers have received during the short period of their continuance in the House, and in not a few cases the assiduous labours and watchings of the attendance have met a recompense in the thankfulness of these objects of their care.

In addition to 58 patients discharged cured, some have been sent home on trial for a month, according to the provisions of the Act, 8 & 9 Vic., c. 126. These have remained with their families in a satisfactory state.

Mental disease has been deprived of much that was formidable by the influence of modern improvements, demonstrating as they have done, that it is curable to as greater extent as other diseases with which the human race is afflicted.

It appears to be clearly proved that of cases in which there is no constitutional defect in the intellectual faculties, and where proper remedial means are adopted in the early stages of the malady, the proportion of cures is as large as 86 per cent. Few acute diseases will afford so large a proportion of recoveries.

That the chief obstacle to a more general recovery of persons attacked, by their immediate removal to an Asylum, is giving way under the prevalence of an improved tone of public opinion cannot be disputed; but there is still too great a reluctance to send patients to the Asylum, until every other means is unavailing. A hope is cherished by anxious friends from day to day, but cherished only to be disappointed, that the sufferer will be restored to reason without a measure so decidedly acknowledging to the world, the insanity of a relative. Thus, the mistaken kindness of friends has unquestionably been the cause of confirming the disease in the innumberable instances. If the advice of those who are practically well informed in the treatment of such diseases is sought, a practised physician would not recommend the removal of all patients to an institution of the kind; he well knows there are moral causes operating on natures of extreme susceptibility, which would render a removal from home and domestic ties highly prejudicial, if not fatal; but these may be regarded rather as forming the exception, than the rule.

Many admissions of the past year may be more properly termed re-admissions, out of 257, twenty-five had at some former period been inmates of the Institution.

When the predisposing causes of insanity are such as poverty, drunkenness, excess of labour, and domestic discord, a return to the like causes is productive of the same effects. The chief alleviation is found in the willingness and confidence with which the patients return to the Asylum, they being often the first parties to solicit their parish officers that they may again be brought to it.

On the opening of the New Auxiliary Institution, its appropriation entirely to the use of female patients was contemplated, whilst it was proposed that the original building should be exclusively occupied by the males. In some particulars this appeared a desirable arrangement, but the two buildings are brought into such close vicinage, that the windows of the one building open into the airing courts of the other, consequently considerable changes in construction would have been required to effect a sufficient separation, and the old plan of separating the sexes in the west and east wings by the residence of the officers and the servants in the centre or main body of the building was decided on.

There are at present in the old building, 190 males, 296 females; in the new building, 81 males, 118 females, making in all 585. Of this number there are

Curable   98
Doubtful of cure   109
Incurable   378

The last year has included in its obituary many of the older inmates, who have sunk from accumulated infirmities and old age. One male patient is still living who was amongst the first admitted on the opening of the Asylum, and he has numbered the thirtieth anniversary of his admission; some few there are who have been inmates from twenty-five years.

To these a sort of precedence is given, a priority, if not in age, at least in suffering, which gives them a claim on the benevolent consideration of all. So far on the indulgence shown by their attendants being regarded with any degree of jealousy, it generally appears to be with the full concurrence and approbation of the rest; nor is it regarded as a departure from the principle of treating all alike whose merits are equal.

In a request intended for circulation amongst a non-medical body, it would be inexpedient to enter at any length on the medical treatment employed.

When the constitution is impaired, as it often found to be the case in insanity, attention to the improvement of the digestive organs, generous, but not too stimulating diet, with as much exercise in the open air as the patient can bear, have been the means by which restored bodily health has led to mental recovery. A constipated state of the bowels is so frequently observed in the insane, that much care is required on the part of the attendants. It sometimes however happens that the loss of sleep is experienced by patients who are not greatly excited; the recovery of natural sleep has produced a perfect restoration of the mind.

Amusements have been less encouraged amongst us than they have been in some other Institutions, for the plain reason that the household is composed of a class by whom they are not readily appreciated, and who having learned to labour for their daily bread, and to find their happiness in the patient discharge of their duty are apt to consider amusement as an evidence or dissipation. Without doing violence to so innocent a prejudice, some of the most morose have been beguiled into the cheerfulness by the sight of their companions enjoying a game of skittles, &c.; the gloomy and inactive have been aroused and persuaded to join in the dance so productive of pleasure to the rest.

In fine weather, nothing in the nature of amusement appears to exercise so happy an influence on those patients who are capable of enjoying it, as long walks in the country. That sympathy with the objects of nature which forms so large a portion of man's happiness in the world is not wholly lost in insanity, and the change of air, the wholesome exercise, and the sense of freedom, cast a cheering influence on the mind obscured by gloomy fears or harassed by delusions.

Of all the means employed for the alleviation and cure of insanity, none can stand in completion with actual labour, whether in or out of doors. The superfluous energy of the nervously excited is thrown off in healthy channels, the natural secretions are encouraged and the bodily functions called into wholesome exercise, whilst the moral feelings are improved by a conscious sense of being useful to others.

There are, nevertheless, limits to this; the insane cannot bear labour too severe or for too long at a time, if it be employed so as to produce exhaustion, the nervous system will become so enfeebled as to occasion effects the reverse of beneficial.

The patients have levelled, cleared, and made the walks and beds of the new airing courts, and prepared the land for planting. In this they have done as much as is consistent with their condition, but no economical project would have justified a further use of their circumscribed powers.

It must be gratifying to all, that the occupation of the new part of the Asylum has given universal satisfaction, although the spirit that pervaded the old was the furthest removed from anything like discontent, yet such advantages are enjoyed in the new building, by its elevated situation and healthy locality, with the tranquillity promoted by its spacious rooms and galleries, that the removal of a patient is commonly followed by a request to remain there.

The patients continue to enjoy a good degree of bodily health, and with the exception of a few weeks during the summer, in which some disorder of the bowels prevailed amongst the occupants of one of the male wards, the hold has remained during the last year in its accustomed healthy condition.

It may not be out of place to make a few observations on the employment mechanical restraint.

That this as well as other Institutions of the kind could be conducted without them is undoubted, but the question at issue is how far such exemption would tend to the well-being and restoration of the patients.

If mechanical restraint be wholly abandoned as injurious, it necessarily follows that a very large staff of attendants must be employed, and admitting that an augmented expenditure would be justifiable, and that so increased a staff of servants might be possessed of all the courage, patience, and good sense their trying position requires, it must then be shown that the contention of a lunatic with the attendant is less irritating and prejudicial than the inanimate resistance of a strap or glove.

Those patients who are subject to manical paroxysms with lucid intervals almost invariably condemn in their intervals of sanity any other restraint than that which is mechanical and are often found to attribute their recovery to its use. The mechanical contrivance acts are quietly, steadily, and effectually, and is submitted to as unavoidable; the mind and power of an attendant are capricious and uncertain.

THE THIRTIETH

REPORT

OF THE DIRECTOR

OF THE

WEST-RIDING OF YORK

PAUPER

LUNATIC ASYLUM.

Wakefield:
ROWLAND HURST, PRINTER, WESTGATE.

1849.

STAFFORDSHIRE COUNTY ASYLUM
St George's Hospital, 1818

The Wynn's Act or County Asylum Act came onto the statute books in 1808, during the reign of King George III, who himself suffered greatly with mental illness. Under the Act, magistrates were allowed to build and regulate rate-supported asylums in each county for the insane poor. The first County Asylum opened in Nottingham. The initial patients, six paupers from St Mary's Parish, were admitted on 12 February 1812. The Staffordshire County Asylum, when it opened in October 1818, was the fifth such institution to be regulated under the act. Designed by county surveyor Joseph Potter, the Georgian-style mansion dressed in red brick would have presented a pleasing alternative to previous asylum architecture, and stretching to over 350 metres, it was certainly an imposing structure. To the north-east of Stafford town, the old building was built at an elevated position, overlooking marshes and set within 40 acres. The building initially provided accommodation for 120 patients. This, as always, proved to be inadequate, and further extensions were added during the nineteenth century. The cost of maintaining a pauper inmate in 1818 was 6s a week, which was met by the overseers of the poor in the respective inmates' parish or town. The external stairwells were eventually closed in with anti-suicide bars after a patient threw herself from the fourth floor near the reception area. In 1929, the asylum was renamed Stafford Mental Hospital before eventually becoming St George's Psychiatric Hospital in 1948, just three years after the conclusion of hostilities during the Second World War. The hospital closed its doors in 1995, having served Staffordshire for 177 years. The years since it closed have had a detrimental effect on the internal structure, and to this day it remains in a dangerous derelict condition.

A very extensive building of brick, with projecting wings, appropriated solely for the reception of pauper lunatics.

External stairwell.

Internal damage after a
deliberate fire in 2010.

Recreation hall – ballroom.

External stairwell showing the suicide prevention installation.

One of the galleries.

The stage area of the
recreation hall – ballroom.

WEST RIDING PAUPER LUNATIC ASYLUM

Stanley Royd Hospital, Wakefield, 1818

The decision to build the first West Riding Pauper Lunatic Asylum was resolved at the Michaelmas General Quarter Sessions held in Leeds in October 1814. The magistrates sought out the best designs for such a building, offering 100 guineas for the winning design and a further £750 to superintend the construction. Samuel Tuke was employed to draw up a basic set of requirements for the guidance of competitors. The foundation stone was laid just six months after the Battle of Waterloo, on 1 February 1816, by John Foljambe, clerk to the Visiting Justices. The asylum was built to the designs of Messrs Watson & Prichett of York, whose H-shaped design in brick, as plain and unornamental as is consistent with propriety and neatness, was judged the best out of forty plans submitted.

By November 1818, the new asylum, built at a cost of £36,448, was judged ready for the reception of up to 150 patients. Christopher Taylor, a hatter, was the first person to be admitted to the asylum on the on 23 November 1818, along with three other men and four women. Although the name 'Mad Hatter' was clearly inspired by the phrase 'as mad as a hatter', the origin of this phrase possibly relates to the mercury that was used in the process of curing felt in some hats, making it impossible for hatters to avoid inhaling the mercury fumes given off during the hat-making process. Mercury poisoning causes neurological damage, including confused speech and distorted vision.

From day one, a strict rule of the asylum was the complete segregation of the male and female inmates. This continued until the 1960s, when the old asylum became Stanley Royd Hospital. After closure in the 1990s, the former asylum was converted into modern living apartments and only the original 1818 main structure remained, along with the chapel. Sadly, the former asylum chapel of St Faiths In Hospital recently suffered a devastating fire, and the unique stained glass was destroyed.

The original 1818 building. The main builders were John Robson, John Billinton and William Pockrin – all from Wakefield. When completed, the asylum was first occupied on 23 November 1818.

The Gothic Revival style church was probably designed by the architect Sir George Gilbert Scott in 1861.

The arches separating the twin naves strictly separated male patients and staff from female ones.

The magnificent stained-glass window, picturing members of various hospital professions with patients.

The remnants of the church after the fire, in June 2012.

CHESHIRE COUNTY PAUPER LUNATIC ASYLUM

Countess of Chester Hospital, 1829

The Cheshire County Lunatic Asylum, which opened in September 1829, was designed by W. Cole Jr and built by W. Quay of Neston. The asylum was situated on the land between Upton Hall and Bache Hall, and was purchased from the Egerton Estate. The principal structure, which until its closure was still referred to as the 1829 building, consisted of a long, four-storey block flanked by two return wings and fashioned in brick with a stone dressing. In and around the front courtyard were horse stables, various repair shops, and a mortuary. The basement area to the front section of the building housed the kitchens, a brewery, store house and laundry department. In the central section of the house were the offices for the medical superintendent, Mr L. I. Jones, the matron, and general staff quarters. The exercise airing courts were located to the rear of the block.

As always, patients were segregated by their sex: the men were housed in the south wing, and the women in the north. Bearing in mind it was 1829, the accommodation and conditions were extremely basic – straw bedding, horn feeding mugs and wooden spoons. Initially, the ninety residents were attended to by twelve attendants and a matron. By 1874, the population had quadrupled under the directorship of John Hannah Davidson MD, the resident medical superintendent. Unusually, the asylum did not have a resident medical superintendent until 1853. During the lifetime of the asylum, the institution was expanded to facilitate the persistent requirement for more beds, and thus a major addition, known as 'the Main', was added in 1896 to accommodate over 400 patients, followed soon after by a structure referred to as 'the Annexe' in the early twentieth century.

A century after opening in 1929, the former asylum had expanded to accommodate over 1,500 patients under care and treatment. Divine worship was always seen to be important, and in 1856 a dedicated asylum chapel was built to allow 350 worshippers at each sitting. In 1855, the first of a number of name changes occurred when the asylum became Cheshire Lunatic Asylum. In 1870, the name changed again and became Chester County Lunatic Asylum. In 1889, Cheshire County Council became responsible for the asylum and, in 1899, the original name, Cheshire County Lunatic Asylum, was restored. Following the visit of the Prince and Princess of Wales on 30 May 1984, the name, Countess of Chester Hospital was acquired. The hospital closed in 2005 and was demolished in the last few years.

A gallery featuring single occupancy rooms.

A single room or cell.

Reflections.

Physical awareness
therapy services (Gym)

A link corridor.

The Hazard Cell, an art installation completed after closure.

Whistle in the wind...

Examples of
the wards.

NORTH WALES COUNTY PAUPER LUNATIC ASYLUM
North Wales Hospital, 1848

The original 1808 Wynn's Act was discretionary and yet, despite the population boom of the Industrial Revolution resulting in the need for more beds, many respective counties were slow to provide places. By 1841, only fourteen English counties had complied, and in North Wales there was no such institution for the care and treatment for the Welsh-speaking insane poor. Those diagnosed as the most serious cases were, in actual fact, sent to English-speaking asylums such as Gloucester. Dr Samuel Hitch, the medical superintendent of Gloucester, was acutely aware of the difficulties that the Welsh inmates were enduring and lobbied the *Times* newspaper. He said,

> So few of the lower class of the Welsh, except in some towns or the precincts of inns, speak English, and this only for the purpose of commerce, or to qualify themselves for duties of menial servants, and not to an extent which would enable them to comprehend anything higher, – whilst both the officers and servants of our English Asylums, and the English public too, and equally ignorant of the Welsh Language, – that when the poor Welshman is sent to an English Asylum he is submitted to the most refined modern cruelties, being doomed to an imprisonment amongst strange people, and an association with his fellow men, whom he is prohibited from holding communications, harassed by wants which he cannot make known and appealed to by sounds which he cannot comprehend, he becomes irritable and irritated; and it is proverbial in our English Asylum that the Welshmen is the most turbulent patient wherever he happens to become an inmate.

Having made the general public aware, the Metropolitan Commissioners in Lunacy were compelled to investigate the good doctor's observations and, in 1844, a report to the government duly concurred with the miserable conditions Dr Hitch had described. In the same year, a 20-acre parcel of land was donated in Denbigh, North Wales, by Joseph Ablett of Llanber Hall for the purpose of building an asylum for the North Wales counties. The new structure, which incorporated a clock donated by Joseph Ablett's widow and was built in locally quarried limestone brick, was designed by Mr Fulljames, who originated from Gloucester, and it was superintended by Dr Samuel Hitch.

Architecturally, the administration building at
Denbigh is probably the finest example of a
Victorian asylum in the country.

Elwyn Pierce, the apparent guardian of the North Wales Hospital (Denbigh Asylum).

Left: The area surrounding the demolished ballroom.

Right: A corridor close to the former ballroom.

During the build, new legislation came into place making it compulsory for each and every county to provide an asylum for their respective insane poor. On 14 November 1848, Denbigh Asylum opened with beds for the reception of up to 200 patients. Over the years, as the population, increased so did the asylum, and at its peak over 1,500 patients could be placed under care and treatment. Later renamed North Wales Psychiatric Hospital, the vast Victorian pile closed its doors in 1995. Locally known as the 'Denbigh Mental', it was the subject of the *Most Haunted* team descending on the derelict hospital in October 2008. In November 2008, the magnificent ballroom that had once been the heart of the asylum was subject to an arson attack, which resulted in its demolition; this was quite literally as locals marched through the streets lobbying the council to put a protection order on it. In 2014, the magnificent derelict Gothic administration building still represents probably the finest example of a Victorian asylum in the whole country.

One of the old wards with the seclusion rooms in the background. The loft insulation seen in the image was used to create a fake padded cell by the *Most Haunted* team.

This image was taken in the basement tunnels.

The corridor linking the hospital to the administration building.

The old projector room.

Due to water
ingress, many
of the floors
are rotted. This
room was no
exception.

Once a hive of activity, this former ward quietly rots away.

The former nurses' accommodation.

It is hard to picture how the old hospital set in such a beautiful was once in effect a self contained village for the insane.

EGLINGTON PAUPER LUNATIC ASYLUM
Our Lady's Hospital, Cork, 1852

Our Lady's Hospital, formerly Eglington Asylum, Cork, was originally built to house 500 patients. It was the largest of seven district lunatic asylums commissioned by the Board of Public Works in the late 1840s to supplement the nine establishments erected by Johnston and Murray between 1820 and 1835. Like the earlier buildings, the new institutions were corridor-type asylums, but with the emphasis on wards rather than cells. There was a noticeable change in style from Classical to Gothic. Designed by local architect William Atkins, when it opened in 1852 it was one of the longest buildings in Ireland at almost 1,000 feet. The building was originally designed as three separate ranges, the construction taking five years. The ranges were linked by low arcades, which also linked a chapel and refectory hall set behind the main buildings. These were arranged so that the gable of the hall and spire of the chapel were visible from the front. The whole ensemble had six staircase towers and numerous gables. In 1861, Atkins was forced to link the main blocks to provide more accommodation, thus giving the building an almost unending facade in the process.

The elevated site overlooking the River Lee at Shanakiel, appears to have been chosen by the local governors for dramatic effect rather than practicality, great difficulty was encountered in providing exercise yards on the steep slope to the river. The vast institution was named after the Earl of Eglington, Lord Lieutenant of Ireland and the construction cost, including the purchase of land, was £79,827 1s 5d. Currently the hospital, which closed in 1988, is partly converted into contemporary apartments and appropriately named Atkins Hall in reference to the original architect.

Situated on the banks of the River Lee in Shankeil, Cork, the three institutions – the lunatic asylum, Cork Gaol and further east the Good Shepherd Magdalen Laundry at Sunday Wells – are known collectively as 'the Mad, the Bad and the Sad'.

The view from the eastern tower.

The stairs are enclosed to prevent suicide attempts.

The assent into the east tower.

The rear elevation taking in the converted section to the right.

LINCOLNSHIRE COUNTY PAUPER LUNATIC ASYLUM
St John's Hospital, 1852

The Lincolnshire asylum, which was designed by John R. Hamilton and James Medland of Hamilton & Medland, opened in 1852, just seven years after the act that made it compulsory for each county to provide such institutions. During its long history, the institution was enlarged on several subsequent occasions to provide further beds. It was originally established jointly by Lindsey, Kesteven, Holland, Lincoln, Grantham, Grimsby and Stamford, and managed by a Board of Visitors appointed by the contributing authorities. Kesteven and Grantham withdrew from the arrangement when the contract of Union expired in 1893 (eventually establishing the Kesteven County Asylum at South Rauceby, 1897). The hospital was originally set in grounds of 120 acres, which included gardens, farmland and a burial ground. The frontage is dominated by the original three storey medical superintendent's house in the main central block of the southern wing, and the three-storey administration block. Both are flanked by two-storey links with extensive H-plan wings to either side, and are of an Italianate design in local 'blue' stone, with dressings of Mansfield stone.

In 1940, female patients were transferred to other hospitals, mainly Storthes Hall Mental Hospital, which was the former West Riding Pauper Lunatic Asylum at Huddersfield, in order to make space for an Emergency War Hospital, which functioned until 1943. Many of these female patients did not return until well after the end of the war. Administration of the hospital passed to the National Health Service in 1948, when the NHS was established. By the early 1960s, it was known by the name of St John's Hospital. Closure finally came in December 1989, with the remaining patients transferred to other establishments. The former asylum was sold in the mid-1990s to a property developer, who constructed nearly 1,000 new houses in the village. The original hospital buildings are classified as Grade II listed buildings and are protected from demolition although remain in a derelict condition.

The front elevation. At one time the area in the foreground would have been magnificent gardens tended to by the patient population.

The remains of the ballroom
– recreation hall.

Left: The patients' telephone box.

Right: One of the smaller corridors.

The following names, among others, were used for the Victorian Institution, sometimes interchangeably:

1852–93	Lincolnshire County Lunatic Asylum or Lincolnshire County Pauper Lunatic Asylum
1894–1915	Lincolnshire Lunatic Asylum
1897–98	Lindsey, Holland, Lincoln and Grimsby District Pauper Lunatic Asylum
1903–20	Lincolnshire Asylum
1898–1902	Bracebridge Pauper Lunatic Asylum
1902–19	Bracebridge District Lunatic Asylum
1919–48	Bracebridge Mental Hospital
1930–38	Lincolnshire Mental Hospital
1939–60	Bracebridge Heath Hospital
1961–89	St John's Hospital, Bracebridge Heath

The magnificent grand staircase.

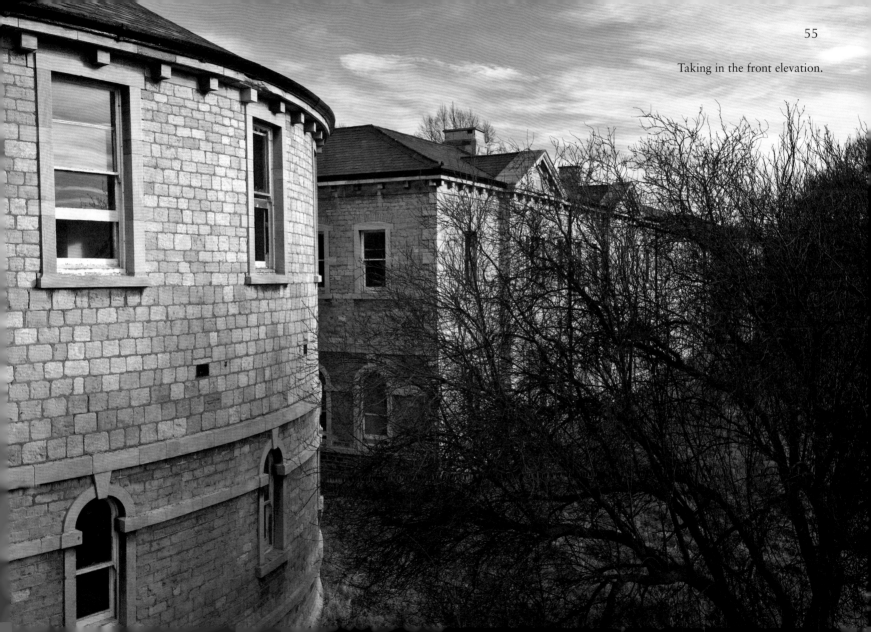

Taking in the front elevation.

Hospital wallpaper.

NORTHUMBERLAND COUNTY PAUPER LUNATIC ASYLUM
St George's Hospital, Morpeth, 1859

Originally called the Northumberland County Pauper Lunatic Asylum, St George's Hospital was designed by the architect Henry Welch to a corridor plan layout. The asylum, which opened for the reception of the pauper insane back in 1859, was built at a cost of £58,000 and saw 154 patients admitted in the first year. By the time Jack the Ripper was mounting his murderous campaign in 1888, the asylum population had increased to 511 as additional accommodation was added. Apparently, in 1890, the rather unsavoury title of pauper lunatic asylum was dropped in favour of the title of 'County Mental Hospital', which was ahead of its time as most other asylums only dropped the lunatic asylum title in the 1920s.

The site picked to build on was formerly agricultural land, which was in keeping with its working farm status within the asylum. Patients who worked the land had to rise at 4 a.m. every morning, rain or shine, either as occupational therapy or to keep the running costs of the institution down. The farm was in operation up until 1974. There was at one time an intention also to have its own coal mine in addition to various other trades, such as cobbler's, tailor's and upholsterer's shops. However, coal prices dropped dramatically and it was deemed impracticable, even though the labour was free. The name St George's was adopted in 1937, much to the delight of both staff and patients alike. No doubt one of the more exciting incidents to occur at the hospital was in 1942, when a German bomber crash-landed within the hospital grounds. The old asylum closed its doors in 1995 and was sold to English Partnerships for future housing and business developments. The new purpose-built St George's Park, located within the grounds of the old St George's Hospital, has now replaced the sprawling, part Victorian-built institution. In 2014, the former asylum lies in a derelict state.

It is hard to
believe that the
hospital has been
closed since 1995.

Many of the old wards are boarded up.

The angel art installation; sadly
this has since been destroyed.

The ballroom – recreation hall.

The loft space above the ballroom.

A patient's view.

A sick ward.

The view from the tower.

A former administration office.

SURREY COUNTY PAUPER LUNATIC ASYLUM

Cane Hill Hospital, 1882

Of all the former asylums noted in this book, Cane Hill, which was situated on a hilltop overlooking Coulsdon and the Farthing Downs, was the ultimate former asylum to explore and photograph. When it opened for the reception of the apparent insane in 1882, it was the third Surrey County Pauper Lunatic Asylum to be built in Surrey, following in the footsteps of Springfield in 1842 and Brookwood in 1862. Charles Henry Howell, who was by this time the principle asylum architect in England and had designed the Brookwood asylum, was employed to draw up plans for the new institution. The architect was also an advisor for the Commission of Lunacy, and therefore an expert on the design of modern lunatic asylums. He effectively designed Cane Hill to be not only the largest institution of its kind but also a showpiece, raising the bar for modern efficient lunatic asylums. The design was one of pavilion blocks linked to an internal horseshoe-shaped corridor. The centre of the administration block designated the segregation of male and female patients. Further segregation included the acute (recent cases), the sick and infirm and the epileptics, as well as the chronically ill. Separate refractory accommodation was also provided for those resistant to treatment. This form of segregation was employed in all lunatic asylums collectively.

Famous patients at Cane Hill include Charlie Chaplin's mother, Hannah, Michael Caines' half-brother and David Bowie's stepbrother, Terry Burns. Sadly, after attempting to commit suicide on more than one occasion, Terry was killed by a train at South Coulsdon station in 1985. David Bowie had written various songs about Terry. including 'All The Madmen'. and the Cane Hill administration block featured on the cover of the 1970 American release of 'The Man Who Sold The World'. When Charlie Chaplin visited his mother in 1912. she had just recently been confined in a padded room. Luckily, Hannah recovered, but it would be months before she did; Charlie Chaplin was haunted for some time by her words. 'If only you had given me a cup of tea, I would have been alright'. Cane Hill Hospital closed in 1991 and was demolished between March 2008 and the end of 2010. Only the chapel, administration building and water tower remain.

Although in a state of dereliction, the hospital photographs beautifully.

Presented
to the patients of
Cane Hill Hospital by the
Visitors and
Friends Association
in commemoration
of their
Silver Jubliee 1952-1977

Silver Jubilee plaque.

The demolition in progress.

The view from the water tower.

Footsteps.

The collapsed entrance
to a ward.

This and opposite page: Browning-Blake ward.

Remnants of a working hospital.

Squibs demolition.

The mortuary.

Time has created a natural roof garden.

WEST RIDING PAUPER LUNATIC ASYLUM

High Royds Hospital, Menston, 1888

After years of construction, the new Menston asylum was to take in her first thirty female inmates on 8 October 1888, all transfers from the overcrowded Wadsley Asylum at Sheffield. Elizabeth Johnson was first woman to enter the asylum in October 1888; she died on 15 February 1904, and was laid to rest in the asylum cemetery located in nearby Buckle Lane. The first sixty-one admissions were all female. It would be November before the male patients began to arrive, again transfers from Wadsley. Like the women, many had already spent considerable time in the West Riding asylums prior to arriving at Menston, and were in the main wretched and worn out, the majority of them destined to live out their lives in the overcrowded wards. Back in those days, the hospital was known as the West Riding Pauper Lunatic Asylum, Menston. By the 1920s, she became Menston Mental Hospital, before eventually gaining the title 'High Royds Psychiatric Hospital' in 1963. When ultimate closure came in 2003, she was one of the last surviving hospitals of her kind to be still functioning. Quite possibly the most magnificent example of Vickers Edwards architecture, the hospital could certainly stake a claim to be the finest example of the broad arrow corridor system. At one time, the institution included a library, surgery, dispensary, ballroom, butcher's, a dairy, a baker's, and even it's own railway. The addition by the 1930s of a sweetshop, cobbler's, upholsterer and tailor's completed what was really, in effect, a self-contained village for the apparent insane. Revered by many, the location has been used for media productions such as the film *Asylum*, and TV series *Bodies and No Angels*, among others. David Dimbleby deemed the structure of such merit to feature in his BBC documentary series *How We Built Britain* Today, in 2014, the old asylum breathes new life, unlike many others across the country that have met with complete destruction. Already, a systematic but sympathetic award-winning regeneration and conversion has seen a substantial amount of the site converted into unique, stylish contemporary living accommodation.

The whole of the work connected with the building and arrangement of the new asylum has been carried out from the designs of Mr Vickers Edwards, the county surveyor, and it will stand as a monument to his energy and skill.

Barden Bolton wards, originally the male epileptic block.

Central corridor featuring burmantoft tiles and an intricate mosaic featuring the white rose of Yorkshire.

The gated corridor, a film prop from the 2003 film *Asylum*.

The ballroom – recreation hall

The stage area of the ballroom.

The kitchen corridor. Note all the plug sockets for the hot plates.

The Victorian Mortuary. The table is now with the Stephen Beaumont Museum of Psychiatry in Wakefield.

The double aspect corridor, a unique feature associated with the broad arrow corridor system.

The clock face and movement that was installed in 1887 by Potts & Son's, the famous clockmakers of Leeds.

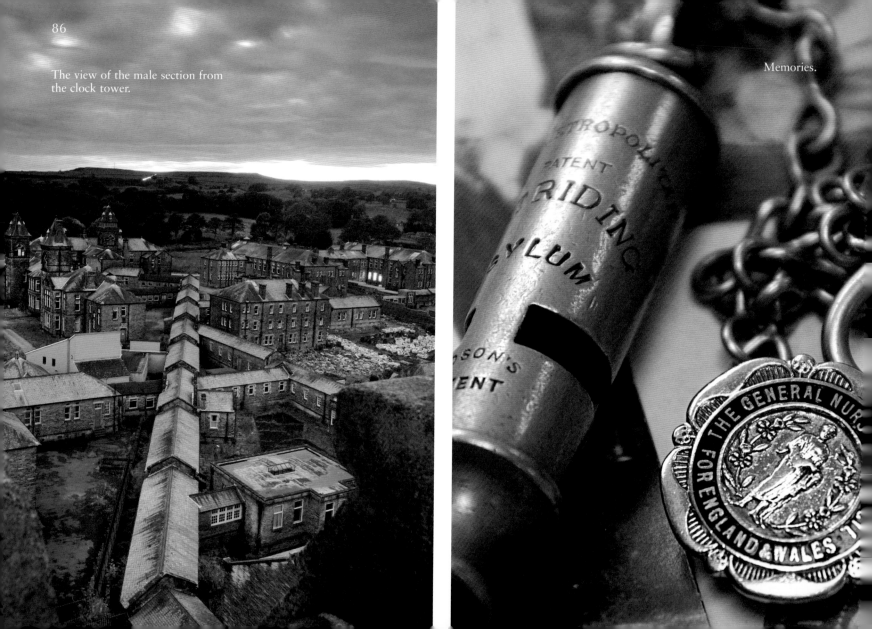

The view of the male section from
the clock tower.

Memories.

LANARK DISTRICT PAUPER LUNATIC ASYLUM

Hartwood Hospital, 1895

The Lanark District Asylum was officially opened on 20 May 1895, and was originally managed by Dr Archibald Campbell Clark, the resident medical superintendent. The construction of the late Victorian asylum had begun five years earlier on land that had been purchased from Lord Deas, who was known as the 'hanging judge'.

Although it was initially designed for the reception of 500 pauper insane in six wards, it was at one time the largest asylum in Europe. The main building with its imposing twin clock towers still remains a major landmark in the village of Stotts in Lanarkshire. Hartwood Hospital, as it was later known prior to closure, was like all other asylums in the UK in that it was virtually a self-contained community, with its own farm, gardens, reservoir, workshops, bakers, rail line, cemetery and staff houses, etc. The hospital boasted having carried out of the first-ever lobotomy performed in Scotland, and further pioneered occupational therapy and community care. Hartwood also contributed to the growth of nurse education, and had its own College of Nursing, which was annexed to Bell College. This merged with the University of Paisley to form the University of the West of Scotland in August 2007. By the time the year 2000 had arrived, the old asylum had closed and most of the wards were demolished. The administration block became the Lanarkshire Media Centre, home to Lanarkshire TV for a short period before being abandoned. In the early hours of 28 June 2004, a devastating fire ripped through the administration block causing the destruction of the recreation hall, dining room and much of the internals of the clock towers.

At its peak the hospital had beds
for over 2,000 patients.

From one clockface to the other.

One of the corridors from the administration block.

The damage after the fire.

The passage of time
has not been kind.

The patient body store.

Part of the mortuary.

Destroyed by a storm
May 1900

Elsie Gould
Dr Kerr's
tell tale

E McGunnigal
Starkhall
Robert Borland
kitshill
Fred Cullen

Water Tank Cleaners
for
Mathew Hall & Co.
Queenslie Estate,
Glasgow.
August 1958

J Boyle
E. McGunnigal

Suetogar

William Bell

Bob Harper
R STURGEON
J McQUILLAN

Big Tam Ken
4-3-59

Matthew
Helptco end

Scribblings in the clock tower.

A view from the tower.

Isolated and abandoned.

GLASGOW DISTRICT PAUPER LUNATIC ASYLUM
Gartloch Hospital, 1896

Although it was in 1889 that the Gartloch Estate was purchased for approximately £8,600 as a site to build a lunatic asylum to serve the insane poor of Glasgow, it would be a further seven years before the institution was ready for the reception of patients. The former asylum is situated on the Gartloch road near the village of Gartcosh. The building, which was designed by the architects Thompson & Sandilands, is fashioned in a distinctive French Renaissance-style. Initially, there was accommodation for 540 beds, but this would rise to a peak of 830 in 1904. The name Gartloch derives from the old Scots 'Gart', meaning garden or enclosure. During the Second World War, the hospital was turned over to the War Office and became an emergency hospital, taking in wounded soldiers. All in all, the hospital served the people of Glasgow for a century, providing care and treatment for the mentally afflicted. Shortly before closure in 1996, it was used in the BBC television series *Takin' Over the Asylum*, where the old asylum became the fictional St Jude's Hospital, in which actor Ken Stott played the part of an aspiring disc jockey. In 2014, much of the site has either been demolished or converted into a luxury village, the twin-towered administration block, however, remains derelict and is awaiting regeneration.

The unique and distinctive front elevation.

A way of life forever consigned to
the history books.

One can imagine how grand this
ballroom once was.

The ballroom stage area.

The view from one of the towers.

ST KEVIN'S PAUPER LUNATIC ASYLUM

St Kevin's Hospital, Cork, 1897

St Kevin's was built in 1897, and was an additional annex to the older Eglington asylum, which is situated on the banks of the River Lee in Shanakeil, Cork. The river, by all accounts, was instrumental in many suicidal patients taking their own lives by drowning. Placed to the eastern end of Eglington, the land upon which it sits is recognised as being a one of the most valuable parcels of land in Cork. Known collectively as 'the Mad, the Bad and the Sad', the land is further shared by the old Cork Gaol next door, and just further on by the Good Shepherd Magdalen Laundry at Sunday Wells. Interestingly, the wall to the rear of the Good Shepherd Laundry is much higher than any of the other former institutions close by. When St Kevin's was built, it originally accommodated 490 patients. There is still in existence a semi-underground communication tunnel linking St Kevins to the former Eglington aylum, although it is in a somewhat dangerous collapsed condition. Towards the end of its life, St Kevin's and the former Eglington asylum came under heavy criticism when in 1988, the conditions at both hospitals were debated in the Irish Parliament. Part of what was discussed is detailed below:

The issue I have raised is the report of the Inspector of Mental Hospitals on conditions in Our Lady's Hospital in Cork. I propose to devote a considerable period of my time to extracts from the report of the Inspector of Mental Hospitals because, even though it is a very late hour and even though I, like everybody else, would like to go home, there are things in that report that need to be put on the record of this House and on the record of the Houses of the Oireachtas. The first thing that needs to be said is that there are about 1,000 patients in Our Lady's Hospital in Cork and almost all of them, with the exception of about 30 or 40, are long-stay patients. The Inspector of Mental Hospitals visited that hospital in February of this year. I want to put on the record of this House brief extracts about a variety of wards. For instance, in St Kevin's 5, a female ward with 28 patients, there was one toilet off the dormitory and five toilets off the dayroom which were dirty. St Kevin's 6, a male ward with 18 patients. Some renovation work was going on in this ward. The dormitory was locked off during the day. Each patient had a wardrobe. There was no soap and no towels were available. The toilet area off the dormitory was dirty and there were no curtains on the windows. We are not talking about prisons or shelters for the homeless; we are talking about a hospital. St Kevin's 8, female with 21 patients — a washing machine on the ward was bought from patients' money, a washing machine to wash the clothes of the patients was bought from patients' money. The toilet had no seat and there were no curtains. Since 2002, St Kevin's has remained abandoned, and is to this day in a derelict state.

The distinctive front elevation which has become a recognised landmark in Cork.

The connecting corridor between
St Kevin's and Eglington Asylum.

The female toilets.

The assisted bath.

The dedicated chapel located close to the main building.

One of the former wards
on the top floor.

Exit to the stairwell.

EAST SUSSEX COUNTY PAUPER LUNATIC ASYLUM
Hellingly Hospital, 1903

Due to overcrowding at Haywards Heath Asylum in West Sussex, a decision was made to build a new asylum in East Sussex. A parcel of land with an area of 400 acres close to the village of Hellingly was purchased from the Earl of Chichester for £16,000 for that very purpose. The new asylum was designed in the popular compact arrow form by the eminent George Thomas Hine, who was the consultant architect to the Commissioners of Lunacy. The construction work that commenced in 1898 took nearly five years to complete. The East Sussex County Asylum was finally ready for the reception of the patient population on 20 July 1903, and cost a total of £353,400.

Like most large institutions of this era and type, males and females were segregated into separate accommodation and work areas. To the west of the administration block stood the male wards, workshops, boiler house, water tower and maintenance department. The female wards were located on the east side of the hospital, along with the laundry, sewing room and the nurses' accommodation. All of the buildings in the main complex were linked by an extensive network of corridors. To the north of the main buildings was a dedicated chapel and four further villas – one for male working patients, two for female working patients and another for children classed as mentally defective.

During the mid-1980s, Hellingly was chosen as one of five mental hospital sites in the South East of England to accommodate a medium secure unit, known as Ashen Hill. Despite these developments, patient numbers were already in decline and the entire main building was vacated and closed in 1994. The hospital remained derelict for over fifteen years before much of the site was eventually demolished. The final nail in the coffin occurred in August 2010, when the iconic landmark water tower was felled in a controlled explosion using 40 kilograms of nitroglycerin.

The once proud administration building lying derelict and fenced in prior to demolition.

Even derelict, the ballroom was magnificent.

Hydrotherapy baths.

CLEANING or LUBRICATION
MACHINERY or SHAFTING
IN MOTION
STRICTLY FORBIDDEN

Part of the laundry area.

A main stairwell.

A former day room.

At one with nature.

BRECON & RADNOR JOINT COUNTIES LUNATIC ASYLUM
Mid Wales Hospital, 1903

The Brecon & Radnor Asylum, as it was first known, was officially opened on 22 February 1903 in a public ceremony by the Rt Hon. Lord Glanusk, who said 'everything has been done that human ingenuity could devise for the happiness and safety of the inmates, and under the blessing of God, for their speedy restoration to health'. The asylum, which was designed by Messrs Giles, Gough & Trollope of London, briefly consisted of the main building, twelve wards, an isolation hospital and separate accommodation for patients working on the farm. In addition to the farm, the service departments included a tailor's shop, a bakery, shoemaker and later a photography dark room, where a photograph of each patient was taken and placed with their respective case notes.

Built to originally house 352 patients, the main structure was erected to the familiar compact arrow plan of the era. The estate consisted of some 261 acres. The total expenditure was £128,710 12s 8d. Later, two female wards known as East 7 and East 8 were added as the patient population increased. The market gardens were spread over 8 acres, and an additional asset was a steam-powered lorry, one of the first ever to be used in the area. This was used mainly to haul coal and other goods from the local railway station. Like other contemporary institutions, the asylum was designed to be self-sufficient, and had its own private water, electricity, heating and sewerage systems. In addition, there were a large recreation and dining hall, kitchens and workshops where the patients were encouraged to spend their time profitably. The first patients to be admitted were mostly from Brecon and Radnor, and vagrants accommodated in asylums in neighbouring towns such as Abergavenny and Hereford. Others came from Shrewsbury, Swansea and other similar institutions or workhouses. After the conclusion of the First World War, patients from Montgomeryshire were also admitted, once the hospital had been extended. Around the same time it was renamed the Mid Wales Counties Mental Hospital. Since closure in 1999, much controversy has surrounded the site. Today, in 2014, the old asylum has fallen into complete dereliction.

The female acute block.

The central corridor.

The purpose-built asylum chapel.

The central corridor, which runs through the centre of the main building.

The ballroom. Note the ceiling: only half of the roof tiles have been removed.

The ballroom corridor.

The grand staircase in the official block.

Exhibits from a former museum located on site.

One of the confinement room window shutters.

GATESHEAD BOROUGH PAUPER LUNATIC ASYLUM

St Mary's Hospital, 1914

St Mary's Psychiatric Hospital was originally known as the Gateshead Borough County Lunatic Asylum when it was officially opened in 1914 in the rural village of Stannington. The construction of the red-brick asylum had commenced four years earlier in 1910, to the designs of architects George Thomas Hine and Hallam Carter, and used the popular compact arrow corridor plan. Sadly for Hine, this would be the last asylum built to his specification that he would ever see, as he died soon after in 1916. Almost immediately after it had opened, the asylum was requisitioned by the War Office for use as an emergency hospital for the war wounded. Upon the conclusion of hostilities, the institution was returned to Gateshead, who added a further nurses' home in the late 1920s. The isolation hospital was also modified to create a sanatorium for patients suffering from the consumption (TB). During the 1930s, a union was formed with the neighbouring counties of West Hartlepool and South Shields which resulted in St Mary's Mental Hospital, as it had become, to initiate an expansion program that was completed in 1939. The wards were, as always, segregated between the male and female patient population. Further, each ward was occupied by a different medical class of patient, to include the sick and infirm, recent and acute, and the epileptics as well as the chronically ill. The exercise areas or airing courts were arranged adjacent to the wards as in earlier nineteenth-century asylum designs, and the parkland, including a large kitchen garden, enclosed the building and courts. When the hospital was taken over by the newly formed National Health Service in 1948, it was renamed St Mary's after the parish church. After closure in 1995, the old hospital remained abandoned for many years before many of the original buildings were demolished to make way for the new community of Stannington Park, a Bellway housing development.

The administration building.

Beds left from when the hospital closed.

The ballroom and stage area, the
heart of the asylum.

The former isolation hospital.

One of the old wards in winter.

Peeling paint is a classic
consequence of abandonment.

A room with a view.

One of the old airing shelters.

A former ward with seclusion rooms.

This area would have been used
to accommodate TB patients.

WEST PARK MENTAL HOSPITAL
West Park Hospital, 1923

When West Park Mental Hospital opened on 20 June 1924, it was regarded as the last great London mental hospital. Although often referred to a West Park Asylum, it never actually came under that category. In the 1920s, across Britain all the lunatic asylums changed their titles to 'Mental Hospital', which was seen as a progressive move and welcomed by staff and patients alike. Although the hospital had been in planning since as early as 1906, building only started in 1913 and was further halted in the latter part the First World War. It is commonly thought that the name West Park was chosen because of its location to the west of landscaped parkland associated with Horton Manor. When finally built, it was the last of what was known as the Epsom cluster, a group of five psychiatric and mental deficiency hospitals on the Horton Estate, to the west of Epsom. The other institutions in the cluster were Horton, Manor, Long Grove and St Ebba's. The hospital was designed to the popular compact arrow corridor system with external villas by William C. Clifford-Smith, the architect to the London County Council. Clifford was no stranger to hospital design, having been involved in the design of nearby the St Ebba's and Manor hospitals. With accommodation for around 2,000 patients, the institution was certainly extensive and, as with all these types of hospitals, incorporated a substantial boiler house and plant room. There were also various workshops, and a large ballroom that also served for recreational purposes. Compared with most of the institutions mentioned in this book, West Park had a relatively short life and closed fully in 2003. After remaining abandoned and in a derelict state the ballroom was burnt down; the hospital was demolished in 2011.

The administration block.

Nature attempting to reclaim the building.

One of the many corridors connecting the hospital.

As part of care and treatment, most hospitals had their own fully equipped dentists.

One of the
hospital's day
rooms.

A treatment ward.

Seclusion rooms.

The vast network of corridors.

The water ingress makes for superb reflections.

A photography paradise.

At one time there were no bedside cabinets, just beds tightly packed less than 18 inches apart.

Many original features remained prior to demolition.

Fire-damaged goods.

A treatment area.

Stretching into the abyss.

West Park was one of only a few
hospitals in the UK to still have a
functioning padded cell.

The patients' clothing store.

LONDON COUNTY COUNCIL

Name of
Institution

Prescription Book

Many original
records
remained in
the hospital
after it closed.

Prior to demolition, areas like this resembled a 1930s filmset.

BARROW GURNEY MENTAL HOSPITAL
Barrow Gurney Hospital, 1935

When Barrow Gurney Mental Hospital received it first patients in May 1938, it was only half built. The official opening took place on 3 May 1939 with many of the planned buildings still not completed. The setting for Barrow Hospital was 260 acres of woodland called the Wild Country, near Barrow Gurney, which had been purchased for £20,000. As the war clouds loomed over Europe in September 1939, all further construction work was halted, much to the architects' dismay. The institution was designed by Sir George Oatley of Bristol to the relatively modern colony plan in which detached villas surrounded a central core of service and administration buildings. Constructed in red brick and surrounded by woodland, the hospital eventually boasted a dedicated chapel, a ballroom, treatment centres, a large kitchen and laundry. The hospital was commandeered by the Royal Navy during the outbreak of Second World War as a Royal Naval Auxiliary Hospital. It was used to treat seamen injured during conflicts or who were suffering from psychological distress, brought in through the Port of Bristol.

After the National Health Service took over the hospital in 1948, Barrow gained a reputation as a progressive hospital in the treatment of mental illness, accepting voluntary admissions and hosting clinical conferences for doctors from across the United Kingdom, but this was short lived. During the 1960s the hospital slipped into decline and criticisms were levelled at the lack of comfort and grim surroundings, and patients complained of boredom and lack of amenities. In 2005, a national survey of hospital cleanliness named Barrow the dirtiest hospital in Britain after inspectors found cigarette burns on floors, graffiti on walls, urine stains around a toilet and stains from bodily fluids on the bottom of a hoist chair. The report, combined with the collapse of part of the ceiling onto the head of a patient the same year saw the closure plan brought forward and the last ward closed in 2006.

By September 2010, demolition of the hospital had commenced, although in 2014 it is still not completed. Recently, amateur ghost hunters Eric and John reported seeing the shadows of small children running into the moonlight and out again and going in and out of the hospital. According to Eric, who was armed with a Samsung camera phone, he had captured five images of light balls. Eric further claimed on a later trip to have seen a black figure with a white head and no face. Given the fact Eric stated he was terrified on the first visit, one wonders why he went back on two more occasions. Having visited the hospital myself three times, I can confirm I have not seen one instance of these apparent ghosts.

John Carey Villa, which was one of the last villas to close.

Welcome to Barrow Hospital.

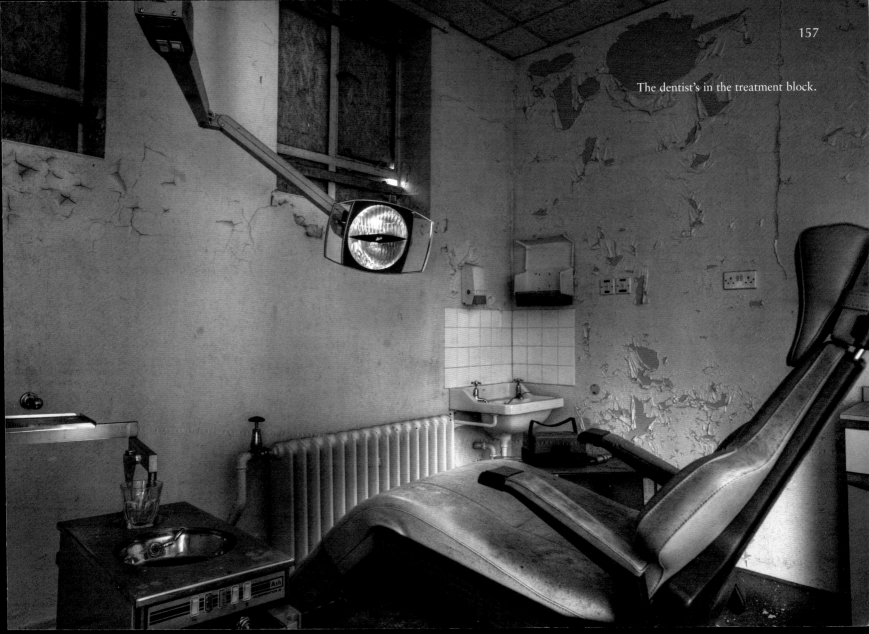

The dentist's in the treatment block.

Welcome to an
alternative life.

WELCOME TO
JUBILEE WARD
WARD 8

The secure unit.

'There they stand, isolated, majestic, imperious, brooded over by the gigantic water tower and chimney combined, rising unmistakeable and daunting out of the countryside.'

Enoch Powell, Brighton, 1961, at the National Association for Mental Health (now MIND) annual conference. It was there that the then health minister signaled the end of the old asylums with his famous 'water tower' speech.

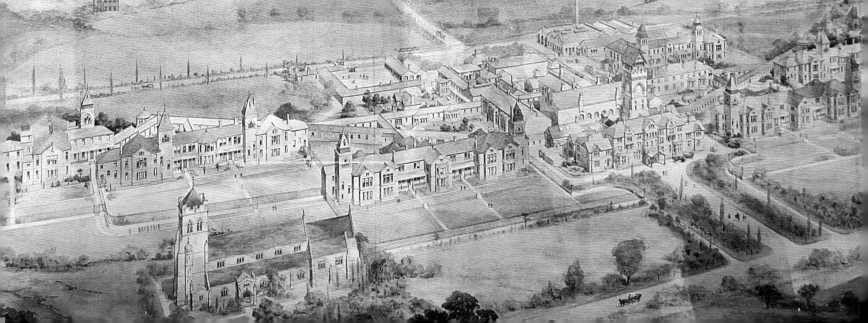